Werner

for Aliya

- for your birthday

love Aaron ♡
2003
Martha ♡
O x×

Werner Bischof

Introduction by Claude Roy

Thames and Hudson

.

On the cover: Shinto priests in the garden of the Meiji Temple, Tokyo, 1951

Any copy of this book issued by the publisher
as a paperback is sold subject to the condition that it shall not
by way of trade or otherwise be lent, resold, hired out or
otherwise circulated without the publisher's prior consent
in any form of binding or cover other than that in which
it is published and without a similar condition including these
words being imposed on a subsequent purchaser.

First published in Great Britain in 1989 by
Thames and Hudson Ltd, London.
Originally published in France by Centre National de la Photographie.
Copyright © 1986 by Centre National de la Photographie, Paris
Photographs copyright © Marc and Daniel Bischof, Zurich.
English translation copyright © 1989 Thames and Hudson, London

All Rights Reserved. No part of this publication may
be reproduced or transmitted in any form or by any means,
electronic or mechanical, including photocopy, recording
or any other information storage and retrieval system,
without prior permission in writing from the publisher.

Printed and bound in Italy

"He saw life steadily, and saw it whole"

Werner Bischof died young: he was only thirty-eight when the Jeep in which he and two companions were traveling plunged into a gorge in the Andes, on 16 May 1954. His entire oeuvre as a photographer fits into a period of eighteen short years. It has a sense of fulfillment, of completeness. There is something indecent about comments from the living on the fate of the dead: to say that "those whom the gods love die young" is to assume an unsuitably Olympian pose. Yet in their intensity, their beauty, and their perfection Werner Bischof's photographs speak of a life that was at all times deeply considered and lived to the full. That he would have done much more in years to come is certain; yet the quality and the richness of what he left behind him make it equally certain that this very patient man, who to achieve his ends knew how to take his time, never wasted a minute of his life.

Had he been a more amenable youth, that life would have been wasted. Werner's mother died when he was a child. When he was fifteen, he announced that he wanted to study painting. His father, on the other hand, wanted him to learn a trade. Each gave in a little: it was agreed that he would be a physical training instructor. A year later Werner rebelled, and was allowed to enroll at the Kunstgewerbeschule—the school of arts and crafts—in Zurich. He was saved. There he found two real masters to direct him: Alfred Williman taught him all there was to know about life drawing, painting, sculpture, and graphics.

(To know when one knows enough is to know what cannot be taught.) And from Hans Finsler he learned everything about the photographer's craft—camera techniques, reproduction processes, layout, photomontage, and more.

His first student essays in photography show him fascinated by natural order and symmetry, the geometry of nature, the abstract face of concrete things. The Neue Sachlichkeit ("New Objectivity") movement in Switzerland and Germany included among its dogmas the belief that "the world is beautiful." The young Bischof and his friend the painter Hans Erni were not unaware of the dark clouds gathering in the sky over Europe; but at this point, on the threshold of adult life and a career—as yet undecided between painting and photography—he paused to make a careful, thoughtful study of the beauty of the world around him, to search, in minute things, for the harmony of the universe. In these early preoccupations he was following a great German tradition that went back to Renaissance painter-philosophers like Dürer who studied natural science, and extended through Goethe's work on botany and the theories of Novalis and the German Romantics on the microcosm and the macrocosm. He photographed maple and poplar leaves, refracted and polarized light, plant stems, the scroll of his violin, translucent shells irradiated with light, drops of mercury. Hans Finsler reports that "he spent his spare time in seemingly pointless pursuits, that would have appeared childish to an outsider; but these studies of different materials and different kinds of light, and their constant variations, prepared the way for his later work." He would spend hours polishing snail shells or seashells until they achieved the transparent whiteness that his photograph required, and patiently sawed through dozens of spirally formed shells in order to examine the structure and properties of the helix. The resulting juvenilia were "art photographs," a genre from which Bischof was soon to distance himself completely; but they provided an invaluable training in composition and the management of light. Many of Bischof's contemporaries among painters, notably Mondrian, began as figurative artists and then turned to geometrical abstraction. As a photographer Bischof followed the opposite path, starting with the skeletal structure of things and moving on to address real life. At the same time, he still thought he might become a painter, and the sketches and drawings that he made are full of movement and a strong sense of rhythm. By the age of eighteen or twenty he had completed his apprenticeship in life: he might have become a very good photographer, probably an excellent painter, a good mountaineer and hiker, or a fine skier.

When he left the Kunstgewerbeschule in 1936 he set up in Zurich as a freelance photographer, a job he fitted in between the traditional periods of military service compulsory in Switzerland, then worked for a year on the famous magazine *Graphis*. He still longed to be a painter, though, and in the summer of 1939 he moved to Paris, where he intended to settle and to paint. War broke out in September. Bischof returned to Switzerland, where he was conscripted. During his two years in the army it became increasingly hard for him to paint, but in spite of difficulties he managed to continue with photography. His work caught the discriminating eye of Arnold Kübler, who had founded *Du* in 1941, and between February 1942 and April 1944 many of Bischof's photographs appeared in the magazine—photographs of objects, of landscapes, of trees and plants, of horses and other animals, and of fashion. They are highly accomplished technically and skillfully composed, and while they are perhaps a little cold they show a development beyond his "abstract" work of the period 1932–1936.

After the war ended he was to find himself a completely free agent, suddenly removed from the safety of neutral Switzerland; he was shaken, disturbed; his true self was born. First as a reporter for *Du* and then on missions for Schweizer Spende, the Swiss relief organization for victims of the war, he was thrown into a Europe of ruins and displaced persons. In a few months, he discovered the sufferings of the world, found his calling as an artist, met the woman he was to marry, and became Werner Bischof, one of the finest photographers of his time.

He felt the sufferings of the world most keenly when he was confronted with those who were weakest, most vulnerable, least able to defend themselves—refugees: men and women with no home to go to, and, most bereft of all refugees, children. Across

Europe, from the war-devastated areas of France and Germany as far as Greece and Italy, from Austria to Hungary, Poland, and Romania, Bischof carried his camera equipment and bundles of warm clothing for those in need, infinitely caring, attentive to all victims but above all to children.

Saint-Exupéry said that "loving someone does not mean looking into each other's eyes, but looking in the same direction together." In 1946 in Milan Werner met a young woman who was looking at the same things as he was. Rosellina was on her way to Rimini, to work in a children's village set up for orphans and for children who had become separated from their families. They looked at the same things together as they walked through the ruins of Milan. (Milan in 1946 . . . I remember that year: Elio Vittorini was living in a house which had been reduced to two walls and a roofless staircase, where only his apartment, on the third floor, remained anything like intact.) Together, Werner and Rosellina looked at poverty, hunger, and lost children. They did not meet again for five months. "We had fallen in love," she said later, simply. They were married in 1949; Marc Bischof was born in 1950, Daniel in 1954, nine days after his father's death. "My life with him was short," his wife said, "but clear and bright as a crystal."

The first collection of Bischof's work, published in 1946, opened with a photograph called "Abstraction," and ended with "Strings of Refugees." Such was the distance he had traveled. The young artist who devised and carefully polished images that might fairly be regarded as "art for art's sake" had not become less artistic: rather, he had become a greater artist, one whose raw material was no longer a shell or the fall of light, a celluloid capsule seen in polarized light or a feathery seedhead, but human beings, life alive and vital. A few years later, he wrote in a letter: "It struck me yesterday, when I visited an old and beautiful chapel, that I have changed in many ways. The chapel was wonderful to look at, but I no longer felt like struggling for hours with lights and tripods to photograph this "dead" thing. Nowadays I would rather go to a railroad station, and watch the movement of people coming and going."

"People coming and going" were to provide Bischof's

subject matter in the eight years of life that remained to him after his meeting with Rosellina: people in camps, people displaced by the Second World War and then by the regional wars that succeeded it, from Eastern Europe to Indochina, and from Scandinavia to Japan. In 1949 he and Rosellina settled in England, where he worked for *Picture Post* and *The Observer*. In the same year he joined Magnum, and those kindred spirits Henri Cartier-Bresson, David Seymour ("Chim"), Ernst Haas, and Georges Rodger. "What matters to me in this cooperative," he wrote to his wife from Helsinki, "is that they are all well-established people, with left-wing sympathies. Two of them took part in the Spanish Civil War. They are free spirits, too independent to tie themselves to a single magazine." Robert Capa was president of Magnum at the time, and active in its head office. Bischof had long conversations with him in Paris and in London, in which they discussed choices to be made, goals to be pursued, and the practical and moral aspects of their work. "Capa can be like a father when you're alone with him," wrote Bischof. He must have been a very brotherly father, since he was only three years older—though it's true that he was a Hungarian and a Jew, and by the age of twenty had a thousand years' experience. He was killed when he stepped on a mine in Indochina on 25 May 1954, a few days after Bischof's death. It seems that with photographers there is no middle ground: you either live to be a hundred or die young.

In 1951 Bischof made trips to Italy, Sardinia, and Iceland; then, having come face to face with the horrors of war, with ruins, and abandoned children, he was sent by *Life* magazine to India where he discovered a peacetime horror: famine. He was fascinated by India. It was the beginning of his love affair with Asia, which dominated his life for two years. In June 1951 he flew from Sikkim to Tokyo, where Rosellina joined him at Christmas. He spent a year and a half there, making side trips to Korea and Okinawa. After returning to Switzerland, in 1953 he worked on a special Far Eastern number of *Du* and on his book on Japan. He also made preparations for a trip to South America, on which he set out in 1954. He left Rosellina, who was pregnant, in Mexico, and wrote to her from Chile, from Machu Picchu, and from other places in Peru—letters as ever fine, full of observation and feeling, simple and direct. Great artists are usually enclosed in their specialism; reading Bischof's letters and looking at his sketchbooks, you know that he remained an artist in every sphere, and that in all situations he was the same man.

Artistry . . . Beauty . . . Bischof was becoming more and more convinced that beauty was what he sought as an artist—but also that beauty is a trap. Faced with the great famine in Calcutta in 1951, he wrote to his wife: "In the last few days I have been thinking a lot about my work in the context of this trip. What I see, what strikes me—these things should be recorded, but not just in an artistic way. What are regarded as 'fine photographs' are often static, and when you concentrate on composing perfect pictures you are likely to fall into the trap of losing touch with life, with its color and movement [. . .] Yet why not tell a positive 'human story' through beautiful pictures?"

Beauty can certainly be a trap. Art can make horrible things look beautiful and tragic things look serene, can make the unbearable bearable. Art can be a betrayal, and beauty a lie. But the primary function of art, surely, is, through the use of style, to make one comprehend the worst. The body that Robert Capa photographed on a battlefield becomes bearable through the medium of his image, whereas a real decomposing body would be horrific. The maggot-ridden corpse of Baudelaire's "La Charogne" exists in a poem: it is devoid of the real stench of real carrion.

Bischof was very conscious of this problem. He had two different, at times contradictory, approaches: to record a given event in beautiful images, and to convey emotion, to try to express what he felt and make the viewer feel it too. You can never, or almost never, know what practical purpose a work of art may serve. Bischof was delighted to learn that one of his photographs had had an immediate effect. His picture of a woman in Bihar holding a baby and begging for food appeared in *Life* magazine and was circulated in the United States Congress during a debate on aid to India: the image hit home, and a massive consignment of wheat was voted by a huge majority.

Bischof was extraordinarily sensitive to atmosphere. In Japan he sought out the measured, regulated, and peaceful world of traditional Japanese life, and recorded it with a Japanese clarity and spareness. "God dwells in cleanliness." When he moved from Japan to Latin America he was overcome by anguish and melancholy, the prevailing emotions in those once-Amerindian lands that have ceased to belong to the Indians. Sadness seems to hang like a mourning veil over the photographs that he took in the last months of his life.

The extraordinary thing about Bischof is that he is an equally great artist whether he is expressing peace and happiness or grief and desolation. But in the case of the latter, his art never consists in diluting or diminishing the harshness. He does not soften or embellish or "estheticize" reality. He is a poet of gentleness and trust—from the Indian dancer Anjali Hora in meditation to the Chinese peasants asleep under a banyan tree, and from the children of Chinese fishermen in the bay of Hong Kong playing in the water to the famous boy playing the flute as he strides along a road in Peru. These images are composed with extreme subtlety. The scenes of famine or of children scarred by war and by adult indifference are also, clearly, composed with care. But in the documents of tragedy the purpose of the composition is to focus attention on an expression of despair that has been captured without violence, on a panic-stricken glance or a figure in lonely isolation; to make us see the tragic turning-point in a person's destiny. The camera angle, the framing, and the lens are chosen to insure the emotional impact of the image, to concentrate our attention and our feelings on the crucial element, a face—the face of the child carrying his bowls of rice and soup in a South Korean prison camp, far below the photographer's eye level and dwarfed by the army cooks as they go about their business; the face of another Korean child, wrapped in sacking, who turns to look at the camera, against a blurred background of uniforms; the little boy in rags, on a station platform, framed by the legs of huge Military Police, like a scrawny cat picking its way underfoot; children seen in closeup, like the Hungarian child with tears running down his cheeks and his chin, or the little girl in Seoul, lost, sad, and exhausted; the drowsy Latin American child slung on its mother's back . . . In Bischof's work, children are the fragile touchstones of justice and injustice. After his death, Arnold Kübler, the founder of *Du* and one of the first to discover Bischof, wrote: "He objected to the behavior of great and powerful men and of dominant institutions. He demanded a great deal of our generation, and demanded no less of himself. He wanted to use the language of form to influence the evolution of the world, for the good of all men." Bischof used children, above all, as silent spokesmen to utter his verdict on the world. It is to them that he turns and listens first—unimpeachable witnesses, judges without power to sentence, innocent, implacable, without hatred . . . The art, in his photographs of children, does not lie in taking suffering and making it beautiful: instead, through the intelligence of his vision and the directness of his emotional response, he organizes the image so that we see the heart of the subject. This is where Bischof's esthetic sense and his moral sense converge. Throughout his life and throughout his work he sought to focus attention on what really matters. He dealt in strong emotions, and was not much inclined to sentimentality. Beauty and goodness are equally matched in his work.

"He gave my life meaning," said Rosellina. "In our two boys and his work I saw my duty, and that has had the effect of keeping him alive. I threw myself into his work, organizing exhibitions and sorting out the archive, which we had never had time to do when he was alive. I concentrated on the past, until René Burri came into my life; since then, we have done things together."

In 1961 Rosellina asked me to write a brief introduction to the catalog of an exhibition of Werner Bischof's photographs, which she knew I admired very much. I was delighted, and wrote the following short piece: "There are several contexts in which you put your eye to an eyepiece, press something with your finger, and stop what you see in its tracks. Among them, I much prefer photography. The photographer, when he is Werner Bischof, is a crack shot: he shoots and brings life, where others bring death; he resurrects the living—trees, landscapes, and faces—just as others lay them forever in the dust."

Often heard as a phrase and seldom reflected in deeds, "love of life" is a concept that has become devalued, but in the work of someone like Werner Bischof it regains its full meaning. His love of life is what strikes one first about him. It is not an empty emotion but an emptiness waiting to be filled. Most of us have lost our ability to see, to feel, and to be truly alive: Bischof's work restores our powers. He looks at everything with wonder, yet with great clarity of vision. The American humorist O. Henry called himself a visual glutton. Bischof was not a glutton, but a man with a healthy visual appetite. It is the function of the eye to reflect; but in the act of looking the observer is himself reflected, mingled with the thing observed. Wherever he was and whatever he was photographing, Werner Bischof showed that no two people see in the same way. His locations and subject matter change, yet whether he is among children stranded by war in Korea or on the austere, stony heights of Machu Picchu, smiling at a Japanese schoolboy or stroking a stray dog in Mexico, tiptoeing past a sleeping coolie under a great banyan tree or treating New York as a particularly outrageous problem in solid geometry, he is always himself. To the person who looks, things are revealed; but the person who looks is himself revealed.

I never knew Werner Bischof. One of my books on China owes everything to him, but fate, alas, kept us apart, and I was never able to thank him and to express my admiration for him in person. Yet I have looked at so many of his photographs that I am convinced I know him. It is the sign of a great artist that his personality comes through even in apparently detached, objective images. I know just how he spoke to those children and how he played with them, and I have seen Korean, Indochinese and Mexican children through his eyes. I know the tenderness of his character because I know how he looked at an Indian dancer or a woman passerby in Paris. I can guess what painters he admired. It is almost as though I'm not sure whether I am seeing the world through my eyes or his. People sometimes say what a shame it is that pictures cannot speak; but in fact they do speak, with a secret yet unmistakable voice. Through Bischof's silent images, gathered together in an exhibition or between the covers of a book, I can hear his voice. What he is saying is that the world is both cruel and wonderful, that life is both dreadful and magnificent. This man who died young, at the height of his powers, continues to speak to us through his photographs and to tell us that life is good, so long as you pay very careful attention to it—which is what he did, never bearing false witness or indulging in vague poetics.

Rosellina's last letter reached me in December 1985. It was written in the same calm, harmonious hand, and in it she said: "Your thoughts and words are always very much in my mind. I am preparing a big exhibition of Werner Bischof's work, and would so like it if you would write the text to accompany the catalog. . . ."

I replied that I would write something that would certainly be fuller than what I had written in 1961, and that would (if I could manage it) be better, too.

A month later I received an announcement from René Burri, the two children of Werner and Rosellina, and the two children of René and Rosellina, on the back of a fine photograph by René Burri (showing the giant shadow of a tree on a parched plain in Pakistan): Rosellina had died on 30 January 1986. She had said in her letter, "This summer I became ill with cancer, which has changed my life." One thing that never changed was the care with which she looked after Werner Bischof's work.

Claude Roy
Translated by Emily Lane

1. Light effects, Zurich, 1936.

2. Deaf-mute child, Zurich, 1944.

3. Freiburg, 1945.

4. Hungary, 1947.

5. Ticino, Switzerland, 1937.

6. Interior of a house at Iglesias, Sardinia, 1950.

7. Peloponnese, Greece, 1946.

8. Reindeer herd, Lapland, Finland, 1948.

9. Finland, 1948.

10. Warsaw, 1948.

11. Hungary, 1947.

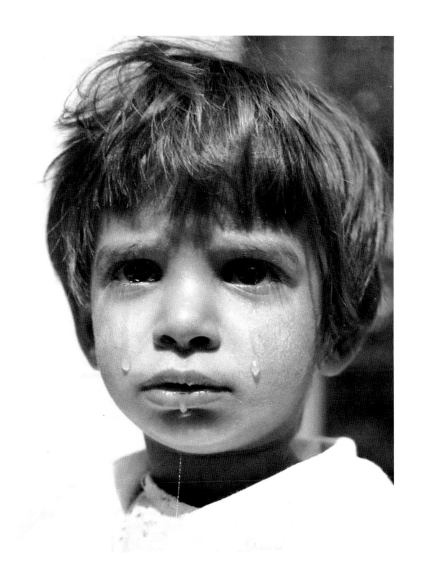

12. In a London hospital, 1950.

13. Steelworks at Jamshedpur, India, 1951.

14. Famine in the streets of Patna, India, 1951.

15. India, 1951.

16. Jamshedpur, India, 1951.

17. Famine in Bihar, India, 1951.

18. The arrival of supplies in a village, India, 1951.

19. Patna, India, 1951.

20. Eighteenth-century observatory at Jaipur, India, 1951.

21. Observatory, Jaipur, India, 1951.

22. The dancer Anjali Hora, Bombay, India, 1951.

23. Beggar asleep in front of the door of a temple, Madras, India, 1951.

24. Shinto priests in the garden of the Meiji Temple, Tokyo, 1951.

25. Tokonoma in a house in Kyoto, Japan, 1951.

26. Silver Pavilion, Kyoto, Japan, 1951.

27. Priests of the Meiji Temple, Tokyo, 1951.

28. Shinto priests in the Meiji Temple, Tokyo, 1951.

29. Iris pond in Kyoto, Japan, 1951.

30. Ryoanji Temple, Kyoto, Japan, 1951.

31. Tea ceremony, Kyoto, Japan, 1951.

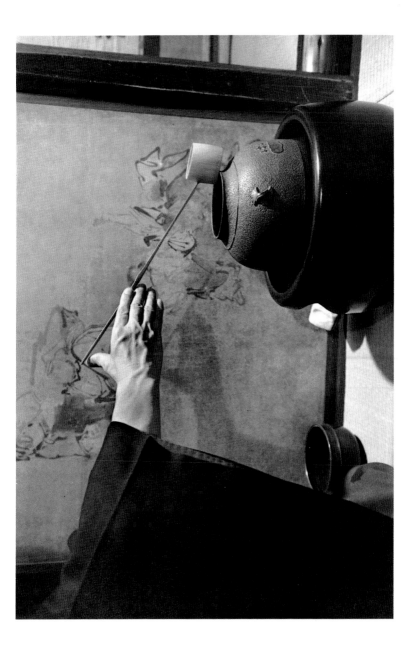

32. Schoolchildren's visit to the Ryoanji Temple, Kyoto, Japan, 1952.

33. Tea house, Kyoto, Japan, 1952.

34. Lotus pond, Japan, 1951.

35. Artificial flowers, Tokyo, 1951.

36. Hiroshima, Japan, 1951.

37. Outskirts of Tokyo, 1951.

38. Music hall dancers in their dressing room, Japan, 1951.

39. Chinese prisoners of war, South Korea, 1951.

40. Busan, South Korea, 1951.

41. Prison camp, Kojido, South Korea, 1951.

42. Gambling and opium at Lai Cham, Indochina, 1952.

43. Grave of a French soldier, Tonkin, Indochina, 1952.

44. Kyoto, Japan, 1952.

45. Japan, 1952.

46. Red River delta, Indochina, 1952.

47. Mother and child, Indochina, 1952.

48. Young Khmer, Angkor, Cambodia, 1952.

49. Women returning from market, Indochina, 1952.

50. On the "La Rafale" train through Cochinchina, 1952.

51. Cambodia, 1952.

52. In the museum at Hanoi, Indochina, 1952.

53. Hong Kong, 1952.

54. Hong Kong, 1952.

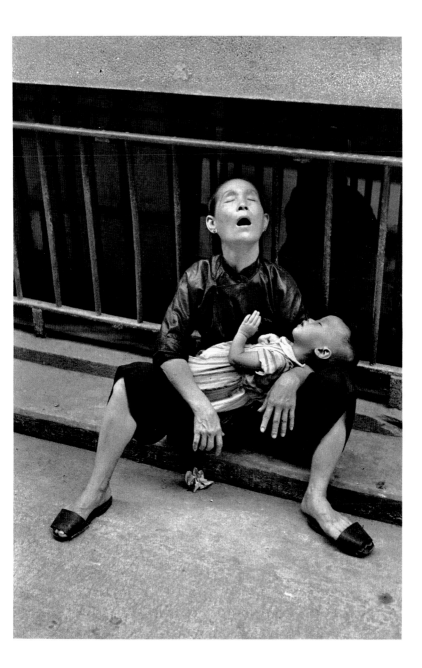

55. Refugee child, Hong Kong, 1952.

56. Cuzco, Peru, 1954.

57. Mexico, 1954.

58. Cuzco, Peru, 1954.

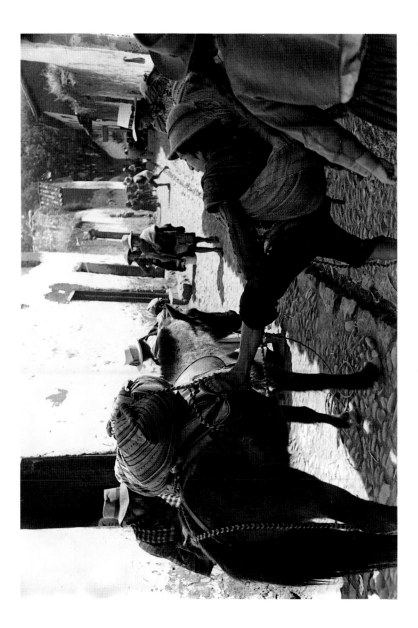

59. Indian child, Peru, 1954.

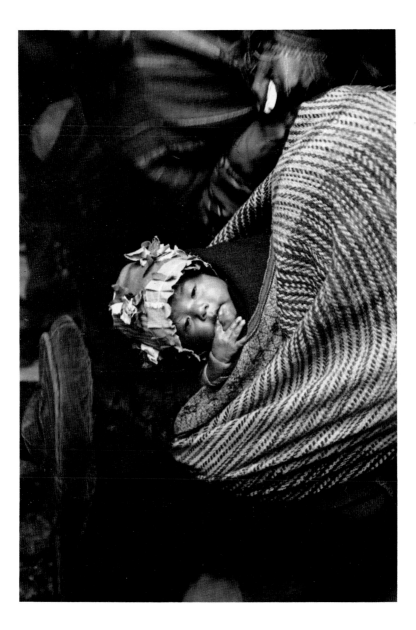

60. Procession, Pisac, Peru, 1954.

61. Cuzco, Peru, 1954.

BIOGRAPHY

1916. Born on 26 April in Zurich, where his father is a director of a pharmaceuticals firm. They later move to Kilchberg, then to Waldshut. Werner shows an interest in drawing and in sport.

1931. Enters the Normal School at Schiers.

1932. Enrols at the Kunstgewerbeschule in Zurich, where he attends Hans Finsler's newly established photography course. Under Finsler's influence, he takes numerous photographs of plants and shells.

1936. After receiving his diploma from the Kunstgewerbeschule and discharging his military duties, he sets up as a photographer and designer of advertising in Zurich–Leiten, then works for the German publishers Amstrutz und Herdeg.

1939. Helps to set up the Swiss National Exhibition: designs the graphic arts pavilion and works on the fashion pavilion. In the summer, rents a studio in Paris, apparently intending to give up photography and concentrate on painting.

1940–42. The war forces him to return to Switzerland, where for two years he is in the army. Experiments with light in photographs that are published in 1942 in *Du*, the magazine founded by Arnold Kübler. Joins the staff of *Du* as a regular contributor, and begins to work as a photojournalist.

1944–45. Photo-essays on "The Circus" and "The Invalid"; then in March 1945, after spending time with Italian partisans who had taken refuge in the Ticino, on "Refugees."

1945. Sets off with his friend Emil Schulthess for France, Germany, and Holland, to record war-torn Europe. The pictures appear in two issues of *Du* (December 1945 and May 1946).

1946–48. Spends most of his time working abroad for Schweizer Spende, a Swiss international relief organization, first in Italy, Greece, Austria, and Eastern Europe (Romania, Hungary, Czechoslovakia, and Poland) and then in Finland, Sweden, and Denmark. His photographs are published in *Du* and in a special number of the magazine *Atlantis* in 1949.

1948. Photographs the Winter Olympics in St-Moritz for *Life* magazine.

1949. Marries Rosellina and moves to England, where he works for *Picture Post* and *The Observer*. Joins the Magnum team of photographers.

1950. Birth of his son Marc. Travels in Italy, Sardinia, Paris, and Iceland. The Italian magazine *Epoca* commissions a feature on "Le Piazze d'Italia" (Italian squares).

1951. In India working for *Life* on what was to be his most famous reportage, on the famine in the province of Bihar. Brief stay in Calcutta and in Sikkim, near the Tibetan border.

1951–52. Sent by *Life* to Tokyo. Spends a year and a half in Japan, which he experiences as a revelation (reflected in his book, *Japan*, published in 1954). Makes three trips to South Korea and the Okinawa air base. Goes to Indochina as a war correspondent for *Paris-Match*. Returns to Switzerland for Christmas.

1953. Prepares a special issue of *Du* and an exhibition on "People of the Far East." Covers the coronation of Queen Elizabeth II of England for *Life*. In Finland for an international Magnum feature on "Women Today." Sails for New York, planning an extensive photographic tour of South America. His wife joins him, and they set off together for Mexico.

1954. Works on picture stories in Lima and in Santiago de Chile, after working for *Life* in Panama. Rosellina returns to Switzerland. Continuing to pursue the theme of "Women Today," he flies to Cuzco on 30 April and visits the Inca city of Machu Picchu. Back in Lima, he meets the geologist Ali de Szepessy, who is about to set off on a tour of the Amazon; decides to go with him. On 16 May their shattered car is found at the bottom of a gorge in the Andes. Nine days later his second child, Daniel, is born.

BIBLIOGRAPHY

Books by Werner Bischof

1946. 24 Photos Werner Bischof. Text by Manuel Gasser. L. M. Kohler Verlag, Bern, 1946.

1954. Japan. Text by Robert Guillain. Manesse Verlag, Zurich, 1954. American edition: Simon and Schuster, New York, 1954; Bantam Gallery Edition, New York, 1961. English edition: Sylvan Press, London, 1954. Italian edition: Garzanti, Milan, 1954. French edition: Robert Delpire Editeur, Paris, 1954.

1956. Indiens pas morts. Photographs by Werner Bischof, Robert Frank, and Pierre Verger. Robert Delpire Editeur, Paris, 1956. Swiss edition: Manesse Verlag, Zurich, 1956. Italian edition: Feltrinelli, Milan, 1956.

1957. Unterwegs. Text by Manuel Gasser. Manesse Verlag, Zurich, 1957. American edition: *The World of Werner Bischof*, E. P. Dutton, New York, 1959. French edition: *Carnet de route*, Robert Delpire Editeur, Paris, 1957. Swedish edition: *Fran Färdevägar*, Int. Publishing Co., Stockholm, 1960.

Werner Bischof's reportages appeared most notably in *Du*, *Life*, and *Paris-Match*.

Books on Werner Bischof

Werner Bischof 1916–1954. Basler Druck und Verlagsanstalt, Basel, 1954.

Werner Bischof 1916–1954. Text by Anna Farova. Statni Nakladatelství, Prague, 1960. American edition: Paragraphics, Grossmann Publishers, New York, 1966.

Werner Bischof. Text by Niklaus Flüeler. C. J. Bucher Verlag, Lucerne, 1973. American edition: Garden City, New York, 1976.

Werner Bischof. ICP Library, Grossman Publishers, New York, 1974.

Werner Bischof. Texts by Hugo Loetscher and Giorgi Soavi. Fabbri, I grandi fotografi, Milan, 1983.

Articles on Werner Bischof

Ernst Scheidegger, "Sechs weltbekannte Photoreporteure," *Camera*, no. 10, 1953.

Arnold Kübler, "Werner Bischof 1916–1954," *Du*, no. 12, 1954.

Leica fotografie, vol. 5, 1954.

John Morris, "An Appreciation: Robert Capa, Werner Bischof," *Infinity*, May 1954.

Charles Rosner, "Werner Bischof: A Personal Tribute," *Penrose Annual*, 1955.

"International Photography in Memoriam: Robert Capa and Werner Bischof," *U.S. Camera Annual*, 1955.

Jacquely Judge and Margot Shore, "Werner Bischof: A Man Who Covered the World and Found No Man a Stranger," *Modern Photography*, February 1955.

"Bischof's Japan," *Popular Photography*, March 1955.

"Werner Bischof and Richard Lamoy Interpret the Far East," *Infinity*, January–February 1956.

Charles Rosner, "Werner Bischof," *Camera*, no. 9, 1957.

Manuel Gasser, "Les photographies de Werner Bischof," *Camera*, no. 9, 1957.

Cornell Capa, *The Concerned Photographer*, New York, 1968.

Virginia Culpeper, "The Concerned Photographer," special number of *Contemporary Photographer*, no. 2, 1968.

"Werner Bischof," *Camera*, May 1969.

Pier Paolo Preti, "Werner Bischof," *Il Diaframma, Fotografia Italiana*, no. 185, September 1973.

EXHIBITIONS

Major group exhibitions

1951. ''Memorable *Life* Photographs,'' Museum of Modern Art, New York.

1959. ''10 Years of Photography,'' International Museum of Photography, George Eastman House, Rochester, N.Y.

1960. ''The World as Seen by Magnum,'' Takashimaya department store, Tokyo.

1967. ''The Concerned Photographer,'' Riverside Museum, New York.

1974. ''Photographes Suisses depuis 1840 à nos jours,'' Kunsthaus, Zurich; Villa Malpensata, Lugano; Musée Rath, Geneva.

1977. ''Documenta 6,'' Museum Fridericianum, Kassel.

1979. ''Photographie als Kunst 1879–1979,'' Tiroler Landesmuseum Ferdinandeum, Innsbruck; Neue Galerie am Wolfgang Gurlitt Museum, Linz; Neue Galerie am Landesmuseum Joanneum, Graz; Museum des 20. Jahrhunderts, Vienna.

One-man exhibitions

1953. Galerie Annahof, Zurich.

1955. Japan, Art Institute of Chicago (traveling exhibition).

1956. Kunstgewerbeschule, Zurich (traveling retrospective exhibition, shown in Europe and then in the United States).

1961. Smithsonian Institution, Washington, D.C. (traveling exhibition).

1967. Musée des Arts Décoratifs, Paris (retrospective exhibition).

1968. IBM Gallery, New York.

1968–69. Takashimaya, Tokyo (traveling exhibition in Japan).

1984. Galerie du Château d'Eau, Toulouse.

PHOTOFILE

The Photofile series is conceived and produced
by the Centre National de la Photographie, Paris,
under the direction of Robert Delpire.